The West Indies

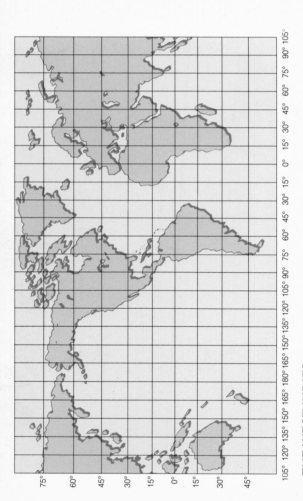

105° 120° 135° 150° 165° 180° 165° 150° 135° 120° 105° 90° 75° 60° 45° 30° 15° 0° 15° 30° 45° 60° 75° 90° 105°

THE WEST INDIES

country	area (square miles)	population (1996)	capital	currency
ANGUILLA	35	10,424	The Valley	East Caribbean Dollar
ANTIGUA & BARBUDA	171	65,647	St. John's	East Caribbean Dollar
BAHAMAS	5,353	259,367	Nassau	Bahamian Dollar
BARBADOS	166	257,030	Bridgetown	Barbadian Dollar
BRITISH VIRGIN ISLANDS	59	13,195	Road Town	United States (U.S.) Dollar
CAYMAN ISLANDS	100	34,646	George Town	Cayman Islands Dollar
CUBA	44,218	10,951,334	Havana	Cuban Peso
DOMINICA	290	82,926	Roseau	East Caribbean Dollar
DOMINICAN REPUBLIC	18,703	8,088,881	Santo Domingo	Dominican Republic Peso
GRENADA	133	94,961	St. George's	East Caribbean Dollar
GUADELOUPE	687	407,768	Basse-Terre	French Franc
HAITI	10,714	6,731,539	Port-au-Prince	Gourde
JAMAICA	4,411	2,595,275	Kingston	Jamaican Dollar
MARTINIQUE	417	399,151	Fort-de-France	French Franc
MONTSERRAT	40	12,771	Plymouth	East Caribbean Dollar
NETHERLANDS ANTILLES	309	208,968	Willemstad	Netherlands Antilles Guilder
PUERTO RICO	3,459	3,819,023	San Juan	United States (U.S.) Dollar
ST. KITTS & NEVIS	101	41,369	Basseterre	East Caribbean Dollar
ST. LUCIA	238	157,862	Castries	East Caribbean Dollar
ST. VINCENT & THE GRENADINES	150	118,344	Kingstown	East Caribbean Dollar
TRINIDAD & TOBAGO	1,981	1,272,385	Port of Spain	Trinidad & Tobago (TT) Dollar
TURKS & CAICOS ISLANDS	166	14,302	Cockburn Town	United States (U.S.) Dollar
UNITED STATES VIRGIN ISLANDS	133	97,120	Charlotte Amalie	United States (U.S.) Dollar

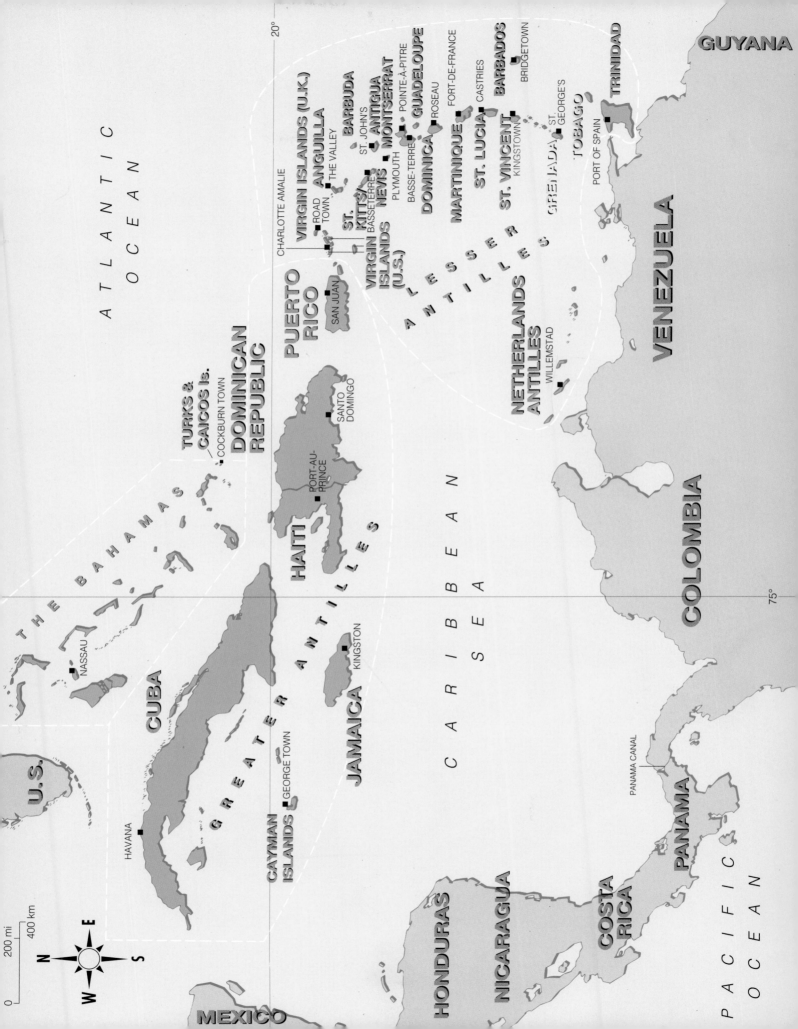

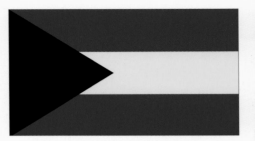

The Bahamas

Barbados

Cuba

Dominica

Dominican Republic

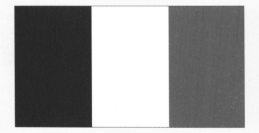

Guadeloupe

Haiti

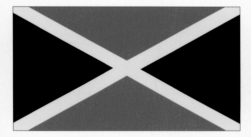

Jamaica

Puerto Rico

St. Lucia

Trinidad and Tobago

U.S. Virgin Islands

The West Indies

Alison Hodge

RSVP
RAINTREE
STECK-VAUGHN
PUBLISHERS
The Steck-Vaughn Company

Austin, Texas

Published by Raintree Steck-Vaughn Publishers,
an imprint of Steck-Vaughn Company

Design and typesetting	Roger Kohn Designs
Commissioning Editor	Hazel Songhurst
Editor	Merle Thompson
Picture research	Bridget Tily
Maps	János Márffy

The Consultant, **Rob Bowden**, is a development geographer
at the University of Brighton. He specializes in developing areas
and has worked in and taught on Africa, Asia, and the West Indies.
He has coauthored other geography books and is currently working in Zimbabwe.

We are grateful to the following for permission
to reproduce photographs:
Front Cover: Robert Harding *above*;
John Miller *below*;
Allsport, page 25 (Shaun Botterill); Colorific/Telegraph, page 20 (Randa Bishop); Comstock Photo Library, pages 26, 33 (Mike Andrews); Howard Davies, page 15; James Davis, page 34 *below*; Eye Ubiquitous, pages 8 (Eric Enstone), 10 (Gavin Wickham), 31 (David Cumming), 34 *above* (Bruce Adams), 43 *above* (Lawson Wood); Alison Hodge, pages 24 *above*, 41; Jeremy Horner, page 37 *below*; John & Penny Hubley, page 22 *above*; Hutchinson Library, pages 14 (Philip Wolmuth), 16 (Philip Wolmuth), 18 (Sarah Errington), 21 (J. Henderson), 23 (N. Durrell McKenna), 38 (S. Errington); Impact, pages 29 *above* (Christopher Pillitz), 40 (Gary John Norman); Roger Kohn, page 43 *below*; Panos, pages 13 *below* (Marc French), 19 (Micheal J. O'Brien), 22 *below* (Neil Cooper), 29 *below* (Marc French), 30 *above* (Philip Wolmuth), 36 (Liba Taylor), 44 (Liba Taylor); Photographers International Ltd, page 11 (Jayne Fincher); Pictures, pages 32, 37 *above*, 42; Still Pictures, page 17 (Mark Edwards); Topham Picturepoint, page 24 *below*; Trip, pages 27 (R. Belbin), 30 *below* (D. Davis); Travel Ink, pages 12 (Abbie Enock), 28 (Abbie Enock); Wayland, pages 9 (Howard Davies), 13 (*above*), 35, 39 *above* and *below*.

The statistics given in this book are the most up-to-date
available at the time of going to press.

Printed in Hong Kong by Wing King Tong

Library of Congress Cataloging-in-Publication Data
Hodge, Alison.
The West Indies / Alison Hodge.
p.   cm. — (Country fact files)
Originally published as: The Caribbean. Hove, East Sussex:
Macdonald Young Books, c1996, in the series World fact files.
Includes bibliographical references and index.
Summary: Presents an overview of the geography, climate, economy, government, people, and culture of the West Indies.
ISBN 0-8172-5402-1
1. West Indies — Juvenile literature.   [1. West Indies.]   I. Hodge, Alison. Caribbean.
II. Title.   III. Series.
F1608.3.H63   1998
972.9 — dc21
97-34953
CIP   AC

1 2 3 4 5 6 7 8 9 0 HK 01 00 99 98 97

C O N T E N T S

Words that are explained in the glossary are printed in
SMALL CAPITALS the first time they are mentioned in the text.

INTRODUCTION

The West Indies, or the Caribbean Islands, as they are sometimes known, are made up of three separate groups of islands known as archipelagos. The largest, the Greater Antilles, includes Cuba, the Dominican Republic, Haiti, Jamaica, and Puerto Rico. The Lesser Antilles includes Antigua, Dominica, Grenada, Trinidad and Tobago, and the Virgin Islands. The third archipelago, the Bahamas, has over 700 smaller islands, including Andros, New Providence, Grand Bahama, and San Salvador. Together the West Indies cover a land area of approximately 92,042 square miles (238,371 sq km), ranging from Cuba at 44,220 square miles (114,525 sq km) to Anguilla at just 35 square miles (91 sq km).

The name "Caribbean" comes from the name of some of the earliest inhabitants of the region, the Carib people.

After they were discovered by the explorer Christopher Columbus in 1492, the West Indies were colonized by Europeans. The British, Dutch, French, and Spanish overcame the local Carib and Arawak people and struggled among themselves to gain control of the islands. They developed sugar plantations, creating a demand for labor that was met by shipping in millions of

▼ *In Port of Spain, Trinidad, carnival bands parade for two days before Ash Wednesday. Some of the colorful costumes are as tall as 13 feet (4 m).*

slaves from West Africa. Since the 1950s, several of the islands have become independent, but many still have dependent relationships with their former colonial powers.

Today the West Indies have a colorful mix of cultures, people, and lifestyles. Evidence of the region's long and dynamic history can be found in all areas of modern life. Many

▼ *A statue of the musician Bob Marley, who grew up in Trench Town—a poor part of Kingston, Jamaica. In the 1970s he became an international superstar and made reggae popular throughout much of the world, especially in the United States and Europe.*

THE WEST INDIES AT A GLANCE

● Population: 35.7 million (1996)
● Population density: 389 people per sq mi (150 per sq km), ranging from 1,549 in Barbados to 47 in the Bahamas
● Largest cities: Havana (Cuba) 2.1 million, Santo Domingo (Dominican Republic) 2.2 million, Port-au-Prince (Haiti) 1.4 million, Kingston (Jamaica) 0.6 million
● Highest point: Pico Duarte in the Cordillera Central (Dominican Republic), 10,417 feet (3,175 m)
● Official languages: English, Spanish, French, Dutch (on different islands)
● Religions: Christianity on all the islands, also Islam, Hinduism (Trinidad & Tobago), Rastafarianism (Jamaica), voodoo (Haiti), and other spiritual cults
● Major resources: BAUXITE, petroleum, nickel, salt (on different islands)
● Major products: Sugarcane, bananas, rum, coffee, spices, cocoa, citrus fruits, tobacco, clothing and textiles, electronic equipment, minerals, oil (on different islands)
● Environmental problems: Soil erosion, DEFORESTATION, water scarcity (some islands)

people think of the West Indies as a place of tropical beaches, vibrant people, exotic fruits, and reggae music. But there is another, less familiar side to the West Indies. Poverty is widespread, and rapid population growth threatens the fragile environments and delicate economies of the islands. This book explores all aspects of the modern West Indies and considers the likely trends and prospects for the region's future development.

THE LANDSCAPE

The islands of the West Indies form a broken bridge of land, some 1,864 miles (3,000 km) long between Florida and Venezuela in South America. The islands separate the Atlantic Ocean from the Caribbean Sea, which covers an area of 750,250 square miles (1,943,000 sq km). It is rarely less than 6,000 feet (1,830 m) deep, and where a fault in the earth's crust creates deep ocean trenches, depths of over 12,000 feet (3,660 m) are common. This fault is an indicator of frequent earth tremors and occasionally powerful earthquakes. It is also the cause of the region's most spectacular feature—its volcanoes. The volcano known as Soufrière Hills, on the island of Montserrat, began erupting in July 1995 and erupted

▼ **The islands of the Greater Antilles are mountainous. Jamaica's Blue Mountains range from the northern suburbs of Kingston to the north coast and reach a height of 7,402 feet (2,256 m).**

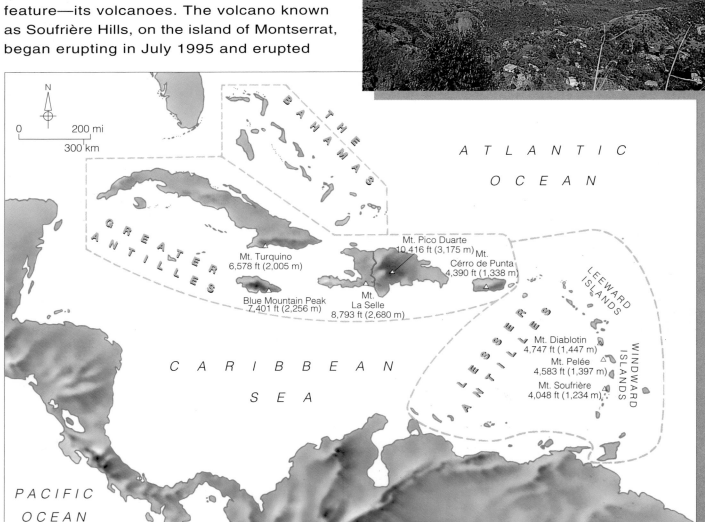

again in 1997. This shows how powerful the forces of nature can be. Many of the islands, like the inner chain of the Lesser Antilles, are, in fact, remnants of past volcanoes. This chain is part of a submerged and still active volcanic ridge.

The Greater Antilles are the exposed part of a submerged mountain range, once linked to mountains in Central and South America.

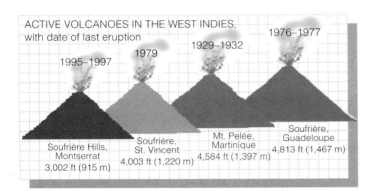

ACTIVE VOLCANOES IN THE WEST INDIES, with date of last eruption

1995–1997	1979	1929–1932	1976–1977
Soufrière Hills, Montserrat 3,002 ft (915 m)	Soufrière, St. Vincent 4,003 ft (1,220 m)	Mt. Pelée, Martinique 4,584 ft (1,397 m)	Soufrière, Guadeloupe 4,813 ft (1,467 m)

Heights of 6,560–9,840 feet (2,000–3,000 m) are common on the islands of Hispaniola (shared by the Dominican Republic and Haiti) and Jamaica, but the remainder of the islands are rarely higher than 4,922 feet (1,500 m).

▲ *Soufrière Hills, one of seven active volcanoes on Montserrat, began erupting in July 1995, sending ash clouds up to 7.5 miles (12 km) in the air. In 1997 most people living on the island were evacuated.*

KEY FACTS

● The Caribbean Sea is about 1.25 times the size of the Gulf of Mexico, but only one-sixth the size of Hudson Bay, in Canada.

● At 24,124 feet (7,353 m), the Cayman Trench between Jamaica and the Cayman Islands is the deepest known point of the Caribbean Sea. Milwaukee Depth, north of Puerto Rico in the Atlantic Ocean, is 30,185 feet (9,200 m) deep.

● In 1692, an earthquake destroyed Port Royal on Jamaica, and in 1907 much of the capital, Kingston, was destroyed by another powerful quake.

● In 1902, Mount Pelée on the island of Martinique erupted, killing 29,000 people —the greatest loss of life caused by a volcanic eruption in the 20th century.

Several of the smaller islands, such as those in the Bahamas, are extremely low-lying areas of limestone or coral. Sometimes they rise only 164–328 feet (50–100 m) above sea level. Limestone is common throughout the region. In Cuba, Jamaica, and Puerto Rico it appears as spectacular TROPICAL KARST, known as "cockpits" because of its appearance. The low-lying islands and limestone plains are often swampy, with mangroves and salt marshes in the coastal regions. In contrast, the more mountainous areas are clad with tropical forests and cascading waterfalls, such as those around Ocho Rios in Jamaica.

CLIMATE AND WEATHER

Apart from the Bahamas, the islands of the West Indies lie entirely within the TROPICS. The prevailing trade winds that cross the Atlantic from Europe and West Africa moderate the tropical temperatures. This means that the islands have a similar tropical maritime climate.

Temperatures are relatively stable throughout the year. They vary among islands, depending on their height above sea level and the effect of the cooling trade winds. In general temperatures vary from about 64–82°F (18–28°C) in January to 77–95°F (25–35°C) in July, except in the mountains and on the coast where it is a few degrees cooler. The amount of rainfall also varies among islands. Generally there is a wet season from June to November and a dry season between December and April. Mountainous areas such as the Blue Mountains of Jamaica receive more than 197 inches (5,000 mm) of rain per year. Low-lying islands, such as the Turks and Caicos, have an average of about 28 inches (710 mm). Flash floods occur during the frequent thunderstorms of the rainy season.

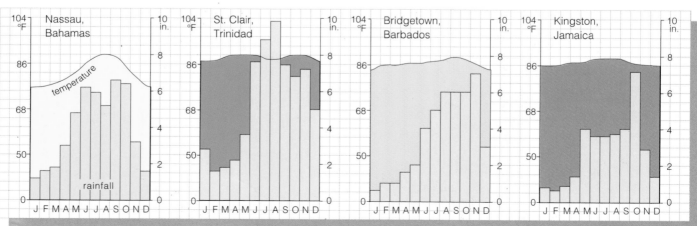

◄ *Cable Beach, on New Providence Island in the Bahamas, is a typical white sand beach in the West Indies. Beaches such as this and the warm sunny climate are vital to the region's tourist industry.*

◀ *Storm clouds building over Havana, Cuba. Thunderstorms are frequent in the rainy season and often cause flash floods.*

▶ **Wrecked houses in Allman Town, Kingston, after Hurricane Gilbert struck Jamaica in 1988.**

KEY FACTS

● In the Blue Mountains of Jamaica, rainfall can exceed 197 inches (5,000 mm) a year. Bowden Pen, in the Upper Rio Grande Valley, holds the Jamaican record with 495 inches (12,598 mm) in 1959/1960.

● Strong winds and heavy rain are common during the hurricane season. Tropical storms occur when the wind speed is 40–75 miles (65–120 km) per hour. If the wind exceeds 75 miles (120 km) an hour, the storm is classified as a hurricane.

● In November 1994, tropical storm Gordon swept across Haiti, causing flooding that killed at least 829 people and left more than 10,000 homeless.

Between July and October, the West Indies are in danger from one of the world's most feared natural hazards—hurricanes. These swirling winds of up to 185 miles per hour (300 km/h) are formed over warm tropical seas and develop in the trade winds, sucking up water vapor to form towering storm clouds. They can devastate property and the environment and cause loss of life and severe economic damage. In 1988 Jamaica was hit by Hurricane Gilbert, which had winds up to 217 miles per hour (350 km/h). It was the worst hurricane of the century. In general the West Indies can expect at least one threatening hurricane every year.

NATURAL RESOURCES

The most striking thing about the natural resources in the West Indies is their uneven distribution. Islands such as Jamaica, with its rich bauxite deposits, and Trinidad, with its oil and gas reserves, are in stark contrast to Antigua, Guadeloupe, and Martinique, which have almost no mineral resources at all. The region as a whole has four significant minerals—bauxite, crude oil, nickel, and salt.

Salt is the only mineral that is widespread throughout the islands. In the past, many of the islands had productive SALT PANS. Today the Bahamas produces the largest amount of salt—about 700,000 tons per year. Cuba and the Netherlands Antilles also produce substantial quantities.

In 1980 the Dominican Republic, Haiti, and Jamaica all produced significant quantities of bauxite. But by the 1990s, declining world prices forced all but the

Jamaican mines to close. In 1994 Jamaica was the world's third biggest producer of bauxite. This mineral accounted for over half of the country's export earnings.

Cuba and the Dominican Republic are important producers of nickel and nickel ore. These are used in the production of

▲ *Trinidad's Pitch Lake produces asphalt, the material used to pave most of the world's roads. The lake, which is said to be one million years old, covers about 100 acres (40 ha) and is 295 feet (90 m) deep in the center.*

KEY FACTS

● The northern coast of the Dominican Republic is called the Amber Coast because some of the most beautiful amber in the world is mined here.

● After Australia and Guinea, Jamaica was the world's biggest producer of bauxite in 1994, producing 9,625 tons, or approximately 9.5% of total world production.

● A US$ 1 billion liquefied natural gas plant at La Brea, in Trinidad, is one of the largest investment projects in the West Indies. It will produce electricity for the island's inhabitants.

● Oil was first extracted in Trinidad and Tobago from onshore oil fields in 1876, so this is one of the world's oldest sources.

metal alloys and plated steel. In 1993 Cuba produced 30,000 tons of nickel ore, and the Dominican Republic produced 24,000 tons.

Crude oil is found in Barbados, Cuba, and Trinidad, but only Trinidad has significant reserves. When offshore extraction began in 1969, Trinidad's economy boomed and people prospered, with the GROSS NATIONAL PRODUCT (GNP) PER CAPITA rising to US$ 6,600 by 1982. However, falling oil prices in the 1980s meant that by 1994, income per capita had fallen to about US$ 3,700. Today oil reserves are becoming exhausted. In the 21st century natural gas is expected to replace oil as Trinidad's main export resource.

Extracting minerals is an expensive and risky process for any economy, but especially so for developing economies like those of the West Indies. Because of the high costs, foreign MULTINATIONALS undertake much of the work. However, this means that a large proportion of the profits goes to other countries rather than those in the West Indies. In the 1970s the Jamaican government recognized this problem.

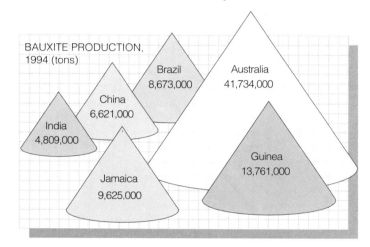

BAUXITE PRODUCTION, 1994 (tons)

India 4,809,000
China 6,621,000
Brazil 8,673,000
Australia 41,734,000
Jamaica 9,625,000
Guinea 13,761,000

◀ *Bauxite, Jamaica's "red gold," is found in the hollows of limestone rocks in the highlands. It is extracted by strip mining, using huge excavators and trucks like this one driven by a worker.*

It bought shares in the island's bauxite companies and imposed taxes on production. In this way, it was able to increase the country's share of the bauxite revenue. But such measures do not always protect the economy. Sometimes the price of minerals fluctuates on the international markets.

This causes problems for islands that rely heavily on one or two mineral commodities.

Besides minerals, the West Indies' other main natural resources are its land and climate. The land is used to grow crops for export, and the tropical climate and beautiful scenery are the center of a thriving tourist industry.

ENERGY

The West Indies have few energy resources and rely heavily on imported petroleum products. Islands such as Trinidad and Tobago can supply their own needs, and a new natural gas plant at La Brea should ensure future supplies. Other islands with a

OIL PRODUCTION
(million barrels per day), 1996

U.S. 9.82

Saudi Arabia 8.9

Russia 6

Mexico 3.3

Venezuela 3.2

U.K. 2.7

China 3.1

Iran 3.8

.130 Trinidad

.001 Barbados

▶ *This is an oil platform at Galeota Point in southeastern Trinidad. Oil was first extracted from the seabed around Trinidad in 1969. This led to an economic boom in the country throughout the 1970s.*

TRINIDAD'S CRUDE OIL PRODUCTION
(thousand barrels per day)

234.2   240   129

139.2   122

1970 1971 1972 1973 1974 1975 1976 1977 1978 1979 1980 1981 1982 1983 1984 1985 1986 1987 1988 1989 1990 1991 1992 1993 1994

degree of self-sufficiency include Barbados, which produces about 45 percent (%) of its oil needs and all its natural gas, and Cuba, which meets about 10 percent (%) of its oil demand.

HYDROELECTRICITY and solar and wind energy are relatively undeveloped. This is because most of the islands' rivers are too small to support hydroelectric projects, although Cuba, Dominica, the Dominican Republic, Haiti, and Jamaica all have small setups. Solar and wind power require large amounts of space, which many islands do not have. Even if they do, it is expensive to collect and store such energy, and the amount produced is not enough for industrial purposes. Much of the region relies on wood and charcoal for domestic energy needs. This leads to deforestation and erosion, but many people cannot afford the alternatives, such as bottled gas and paraffin.

◄ *A hydroelectric dam at Pelgré in Haiti. Deforestation and subsequent erosion along the river that feeds the dam has caused the reservoir to fill up with topsoil—a process known as siltation.*

17

POPULATION

In 1996 the population of the West Indies was approximately 36 million, with 90% living on just five islands—Cuba, the Dominican Republic, Haiti, Puerto Rico, and Jamaica. Cuba, the most heavily populated island, has nearly 11 million people, compared with Anguilla, which has only 10,400 inhabitants. Because the size of the population is significant relative to the size of the island, population density is a better measure of how populated each island is. This ranges from 49 people per square mile (19 people per square km) in the Bahamas to 1,549 per square mile (598 per sq km) in Barbados.

The population of the West Indies is growing at an average of 1.5–2.0% per year.

▲ **Squatter settlements like this one in Haiti are home to many of the poorest people in the West Indies. They lack services like electricity, running water, a sewer system, and garbage collection.**

POPULATION
annual growth rate,
1980–1995 (%)

Growth rate	Country
0.7	Anguilla
0.9	Cuba
2.1	Dominican Republic
2	Haiti
0.9	Jamaica
1.3	Trinidad & Tobago
1	U.S.
0.2	U.K.

▶ **Children in a slum in Havana, Cuba. A high percentage of the population in this region are under the age of 15.**

This means it will double in 34 to 46 years, if these rates continue. Some islands such as Grenada, Haiti, and St. Lucia have over 40% of their population under the age of 15. When these young people have children of their own, the rate of population growth will increase considerably. By contrast, only about 25% of the population in Cuba,

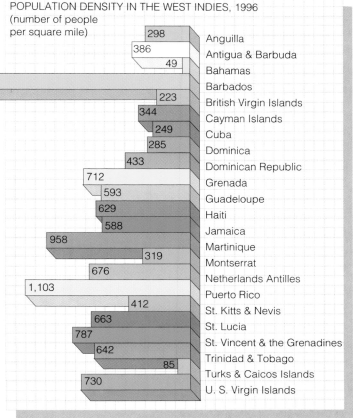

POPULATION DENSITY IN THE WEST INDIES, 1996
(number of people per square mile)

298	Anguilla
386	Antigua & Barbuda
49	Bahamas
1,549	Barbados
223	British Virgin Islands
344	Cayman Islands
249	Cuba
285	Dominica
433	Dominican Republic
712	Grenada
593	Guadeloupe
629	Haiti
588	Jamaica
958	Martinique
319	Montserrat
676	Netherlands Antilles
1,103	Puerto Rico
412	St. Kitts & Nevis
663	St. Lucia
787	St. Vincent & the Grenadines
642	Trinidad & Tobago
85	Turks & Caicos Islands
730	U. S. Virgin Islands

Barbados, and Martinique are under 15. But this is still a higher proportion than in North America and Europe, where the figure is about 20%.

ETHNIC GROUPS AND LANGUAGES

The long and changing history of the West Indies is largely responsible for its truly COSMOPOLITAN population of today. The native Carib and Arawak people were largely wiped out with the arrival of the Europeans in the 16th century. The islands soon became populated with millions of West Africans who were shipped over as slaves for European sugar plantations. When slavery was eventually abolished in the 19th century, the African immigrants rebelled and the Europeans turned to India and China to supply INDENTURED LABORERS for their estates.

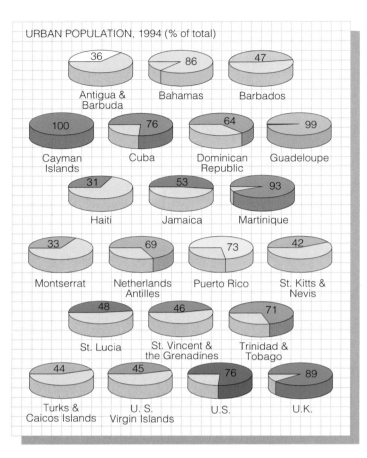

URBAN POPULATION, 1994 (% of total)

Location	%
Antigua & Barbuda	36
Bahamas	86
Barbados	47
Cayman Islands	100
Cuba	76
Dominican Republic	64
Guadeloupe	99
Haiti	31
Jamaica	53
Martinique	93
Montserrat	33
Netherlands Antilles	69
Puerto Rico	73
St. Kitts & Nevis	42
St. Lucia	48
St. Vincent & the Grenadines	46
Trinidad & Tobago	71
Turks & Caicos Islands	44
U.S. Virgin Islands	45
U.S.	76
U.K.	89

Immigration from India was particularly high. These workers became known as East Indians to distinguish them from the West Indians already living in the West Indies. All these periods of history are reflected in the cosmopolitan population of the region, and nowhere more so than in Trinidad and Tobago. These islands are among the most ethnically diverse countries in the world. Many of today's population are of mixed race, such as the Afro-Europeans or Afro-East Indians. In the Dominican Republic, mixed races account for 73% of the population. The major languages in the region are English, Spanish, and Creole. French and Dutch are spoken on islands such as Martinique and the Netherlands Antilles. Creole is a language that was developed to make it possible for people from several language groups to communicate in a common language. In the West Indies, its origins can be traced to English, French, and Spanish.

◀ *A unique feature of the waterfront in Willemstad, Curaçao, in the Netherlands Antilles. Dutch settlers built the 17th-century buildings.*

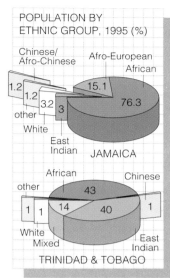

POPULATION BY
ETHNIC GROUP, 1995 (%)

Chinese/
Afro-Chinese

Afro-European

African

1.2

1.2 3.2 3

15.1

76.3

other

White

East
Indian

JAMAICA

African

Chinese

other

43

1 1 14 40 1

White

Mixed

East
Indian

TRINIDAD & TOBAGO

KEY FACTS

● In 1996 the West Indian population was estimated to be 35,710,000, which is about twice the population of New York State.

● Average population density in the West Indies is 385 people per square mile (150 per sq km), compared with 176 per square mile (68 per sq km) in Europe and 73 per square mile (28 per sq km) in the U.S.

● Haiti has only 1 doctor for every 7,000 people, compared with the U.S., which has 1 doctor for every 444 people.

▲ *A Carnival street parade at Castries, St. Lucia. The Caribbean is home to people from many different ethnic backgrounds.*

MIGRATION

West Indian people are nearly all descended from migrants, and today they are still a population on the move. In the early 20th century, many left to find work and helped in the building of America's railroads and the construction of the Panama Canal, which links the Atlantic and Pacific oceans. In the 1950s, thousands of West Indians migrated to the United Kingdom to fill a demand for workers in hospitals, restaurants, and public transportation. Of the 12,000 people living in Montserrat at the time, 4,000 emigrated; by 1970, 300,000 Jamaicans (about 15% of the population) had moved to the U.K. Although emigration eased pressures in the islands and provided valuable income, since people sent money home, it also led to a more harmful "brain drain" of skilled people such as doctors and teachers, a situation that continues today. Immigration to the West Indies is generally low, although the Bahamas and the U.S. Virgin Islands attract people from neighboring islands with their higher standard of living and low taxes.

DAILY LIFE

This old board house in Jamaica is typical of rural housing in the West Indies.

▼ Luxury residential areas such as this one in Kingston, Jamaica, are home to a small proportion of the population. Many of them have satellite dishes, and swimming pools and employ domestic workers.

Daily life in the West Indies varies greatly from island to island. Haiti, for example, is the poorest nation in the Western Hemisphere, with a 1995 per capita income of just US$ 250, while the Cayman Islands enjoy a per capita income of about US$ 22,500. This is more than in the U.K. or Canada. On Guadeloupe, 99% of the population live in towns and cities, but the urban population is only 36% in Antigua and Barbuda.

URBAN LIFE

Over the whole region, 60 percent of the population live in towns and cities, working in offices, banks, stores, and restaurants, on public transportation, and in the hotel and tourism industry. The banking sector is particularly important, and many people earn high incomes and can afford to live in luxurious houses with cars and household workers. The majority earn low incomes and live in cramped and often low-quality housing.

RURAL LIFE

The majority of poor West Indians live in rural areas. It is no coincidence that Haiti, with the highest proportion of rural population at about 70%, is also the poorest, with an estimated 76% of the population living in poverty. Most who live in rural areas farm

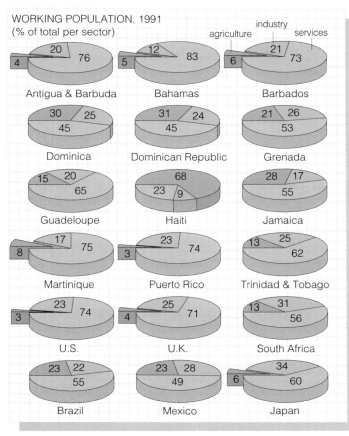

WORKING POPULATION, 1991
(% of total per sector)

agriculture — industry — services

Antigua & Barbuda	Bahamas	Barbados
20 / 76 / 4	12 / 83 / 5	21 / 73 / 6
Dominica	Dominican Republic	Grenada
30 / 25 / 45	31 / 24 / 45	21 / 26 / 53
Guadeloupe	Haiti	Jamaica
15 / 20 / 65	68 / 23 / 9	28 / 17 / 55
Martinique	Puerto Rico	Trinidad & Tobago
17 / 75 / 8	23 / 74 / 3	13 / 25 / 62
U.S.	U.K.	South Africa
23 / 74 / 3	25 / 71 / 4	13 / 31 / 56
Brazil	Mexico	Japan
23 / 22 / 55	23 / 28 / 49	34 / 60 / 6

their own land or work on plantations producing export crops such as sugarcane and bananas. Children are an important part of the rural economy, helping around the house, in the fields, and by taking produce to markets.

EDUCATION

Throughout the West Indies, education is free and compulsory for children up to about 11 or 12 years old. On some islands, such as Barbados, it is compulsory up to the age of 16. The proportion of children who complete primary schooling varies dramatically, from over 95% in Jamaica and Trinidad and Tobago to just 47% in Haiti—one of the lowest rates in the world. Enrollment in secondary schools also varies, at only 22% in Haiti, compared with about 75% in Trinidad and Tobago. With the exception of Haiti, the large numbers of children attending school are responsible

◀ *Dominoes is a popular pastime in the West Indies. These players are in Santo Domingo, in the Dominican Republic.*

▶ *Primary education is free and compulsory on most of the islands. These Jamaican girls work and play during their lunchtime break.*

ADULT LITERACY RATE, 1995 (%)

Country	Rate
Anguilla	95
Antigua & Barbuda	95
Bahamas	98
Barbados	97
British Virgin Islands	98
Cayman Islands	98
Cuba	95
Dominica	94
Dominican Republic	82
Grenada	98
Guadeloupe	90
Haiti	45
Jamaica	85
Martinique	93
Montserrat	97
Netherlands Antilles	98
Puerto Rico	89
St. Kitts & Nevis	90
St. Lucia	82
St. Vincent & the Grenadines	82
Trinidad & Tobago	98
Turks & Caicos Islands	98
U.S.	95
U.K.	95

▼ *A church service in Bridgetown, Barbados. Churchgoing plays an important part in many people's lives, especially in rural areas.*

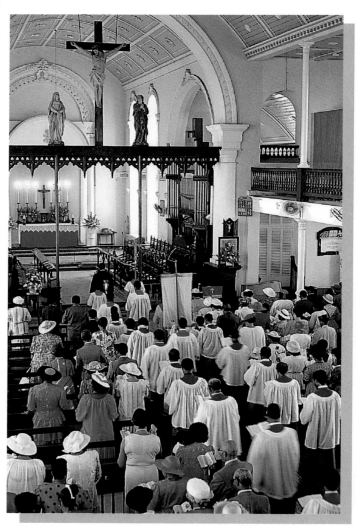

for the high adult literacy rates in the West Indies. These are above those of many other developing parts of the world.

RELIGION

Christianity is the main religion of the West Indies, although it is split into many denominations. Hinduism and Islam are significant on islands with East Indian communities, like Trinidad where 25% of the population are Hindus and 6% Muslims.

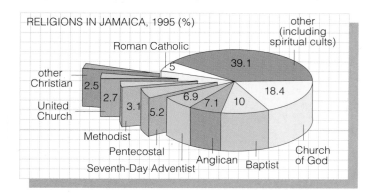

RELIGIONS IN JAMAICA, 1995 (%)

- other (including spiritual cults) 39.1
- Church of God 18.4
- Baptist 10
- Anglican 7.1
- Seventh-Day Adventist 6.9
- Pentecostal 5.2
- Methodist 3.1
- United Church 2.7
- other Christian 2.5
- Roman Catholic 5

There are also spiritual religions related to African beliefs, like voodoo in Haiti. In Jamaica, the Rastafarian religion has a strong following.

▲ *The West Indies have produced many world-class cricketers like Sir Gary Sobers, Viv Richards, and Brian Lara. This match in St. Kitts was played during an Australian tour to the West Indies.*

KEY FACTS

● The reggae group Bob Marley and the Wailers were so influential that they even played in Zimbabwe's independence ceremony in 1980. Sadly, Bob Marley died the following year of cancer at only age 36.

● The oldest university in the Western Hemisphere, the Autonomous University of Santo Domingo, was founded in the Dominican Republic in 1538.

● The 1992 Nobel Prize for Literature was won by Derek Walcott, a St. Lucian poet.

● Brian Lara, a cricket player from Trinidad, holds the world record for the highest ever innings (501 not out) and the highest test innings (375) for the West Indies against England.

CULTURAL LIFE AND SPORTS

Music and dance are central to West Indian culture, and the strong Caribbean rhythms have influenced musicians all over the world. Reggae music is the most famous. Trinidad is the home of calypso music, and in the 1930s its musicians turned old oil barrels into musical drums to give birth to the music of steel bands. The influence of West African culture is strong, particularly so in Trinidad's world-famous carnival.

Cricket is the most widely played sport, and the West Indies team is among the finest in the world. The islands have also produced the world's greatest sprinters, with the last three Olympic (100 meters) champions being Jamaican born, including Donovan Bailey (running for Canada), who broke the world record in the 1996 Olympic Games.

RULES AND LAWS

COLONIALISM

The modern West Indies is characterized by a true mixture of ruling powers and political systems, but there is one element all the islands have shared—colonialism. In the 17th and 18th centuries, Great Britain, France, Spain, the Netherlands, and Denmark all struggled for a share of the West Indies. Some islands changed hands several times. Tobago, for example, was occupied by the British, Dutch, and French during the 17th century. The U.S. also intervened, taking control of Puerto Rico after the Spanish-American War of 1898. In 1917 the U.S. bought the Virgin Islands from the Danish for US$ 25 million. The islands provided a naval base to protect shipping traffic between the Atlantic Ocean and the Panama Canal.

▲ *Government House, Nassau, in the Bahamas. The Bahamas is one of eight parliamentary monarchies in the West Indies whose governments are modeled after the British form of government.*

INDEPENDENCE

Haiti was the first of the islands to gain independence in 1804, following a successful revolt by former slaves against the French. The Spanish colonies of the Dominican Republic and Cuba followed in 1865 and 1898, respectively. There were no further changes until after World War II. Then, in 1946, the French islands (Guadeloupe and Martinique) were made part of France itself, and in 1954 the Dutch made the Netherlands Antilles a dependency.

The British gave independence to Jamaica and Trinidad and Tobago in 1962, and later to most of their other colonies. Eight of them became parliamentary monarchies, with the British monarch as their head of state, while two (Dominica and Trinidad and Tobago) became parliamentary republics with an elected President. All of them became members of the Commonwealth. Five of the former British colonies, including the Cayman Islands and Montserrat, are now dependent territories. This means they are represented by a Governor, who manages most of their internal affairs. Great Britain, however, is still responsible for foreign policy and defense, and the British monarch remains the head of state.

THE REPUBLICS

There are three West Indian republics with elected Presidents as their heads of state. Cuba is a one-party Communist state, which means that, although there are elections, the candidates are all representatives of the Communist party. The Dominican Republic and Haiti are both democracies with several parties, but they have been plagued by oppressive dictators and COUPS D'ÉTAT. The U.S. has intervened in the politics of both islands on several occasions, most recently sending troops into the Dominican Republic in 1965.

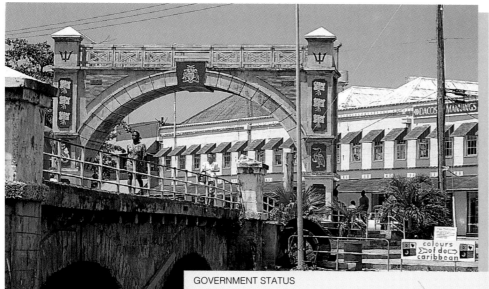

▲ *Independence Arch, Bridgetown, Barbados. The island achieved independence from Great Britain in 1966.*

GOVERNMENT STATUS

Country	Status	Since	Former status
ANGUILLA	British Dependent Territory	1982	British colony
ANTIGUA & BARBUDA	Parliamentary monarchy	1981	British colony
BAHAMAS	Parliamentary monarchy	1973	British colony
BARBADOS	Parliamentary monarchy	1966	British colony
BRITISH VIRGIN ISLANDS	British Dependent Territory	1960	British colony
CAYMAN ISLANDS	British Dependent Territory	1962	British colony
CUBA	Republic	1898	Spanish colony
DOMINICA	Parliamentary republic	1978	British colony
DOMINICAN REPUBLIC	Republic	1865	Spanish colony
GRENADA	Parliamentary monarchy	1974	British colony
GUADELOUPE	Overseas Department of France	1946	French colony
HAITI	Republic	1804	French colony
JAMAICA	Parliamentary monarchy	1962	British colony
MARTINIQUE	Overseas Department of France	1946	French colony
MONTSERRAT	British Dependent Territory	1960	British colony
NETHERLANDS ANTILLES	Netherlands Dependencies	1954	Dutch colony
PUERTO RICO	Self-governing commonwealth	1952	U.S. possession
ST. KITTS & NEVIS	Parliamentary monarchy	1983	British colony
ST. LUCIA	Parliamentary monarchy	1979	British colony
ST. VINCENT & THE GRENADINES	Parliamentary monarchy	1979	British colony
TRINIDAD & TOBAGO	Parliamentary republic	1962	British colony
TURKS & CAICOS ISLANDS	British Dependent Territory	1972	British colony
U.S. VIRGIN ISLANDS	U.S. External Territory	1917	Danish colony

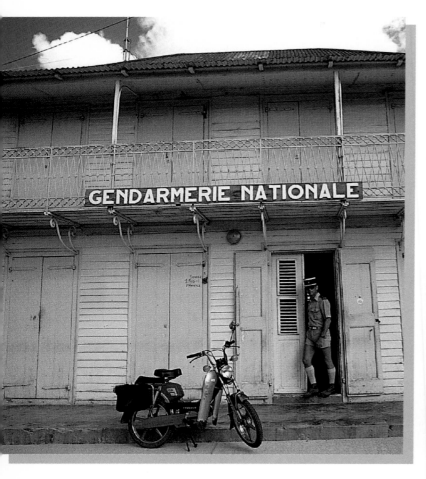

▼ *A policeman emerges from a national police station in Terre-de-Haut, Guadeloupe. Guadeloupe is governed as a district of France.*

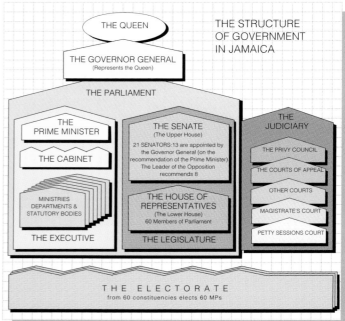

THE QUEEN

THE GOVERNOR GENERAL
(Represents the Queen)

THE STRUCTURE OF GOVERNMENT IN JAMAICA

THE PARLIAMENT

THE PRIME MINISTER

THE CABINET

MINISTRIES DEPARTMENTS & STATUTORY BODIES

THE EXECUTIVE

THE SENATE
(The Upper House)
21 SENATORS:13 are appointed by the Governor General (on the recommendation of the Prime Minister) The Leader of the Opposition recommends 8

THE HOUSE OF REPRESENTATIVES
(The Lower House)
60 Members of Parliament

THE LEGISLATURE

THE JUDICIARY

THE PRIVY COUNCIL

THE COURTS OF APPEAL

OTHER COURTS

MAGISTRATE'S COURT

PETTY SESSIONS COURT

THE ELECTORATE
from 60 constituencies elects 60 MPs

In 1994 the U.S. sent troops into Haiti to restore stability and democracy.

OVERSEAS CONNECTIONS

Largely due to their colonial history, the modern states of the West Indies maintain close overseas connections. The Netherlands Antilles maintain a Dutch legal system, the people of Guadeloupe and Martinique have the same rights and obligations as French citizens, and the former British colonies operate legal systems based on English Law. Puerto Rico

KEY FACTS

● In 1804 Haiti became the first Caribbean country to achieve independence and the first black republic in the world.
● In 1983 and 1994, U.S. troops invaded Grenada and Haiti following coups d'état.
● In 1958 most British West Indian islands formed the Federation of the West Indies. It did not survive: in 1962, Jamaica and Trinidad and Tobago became independent.
● The age of voting is 18 in all of the West Indies except Cuba, where people can vote at age 16.
● In the early 1980s, the U.S. Embassy estimated that Jamaica earned US$ 1.5 billion from the illegal export of marijuana. This led to a major clampdown on illegal producers on the island.
● Puerto Ricans share most of the rights of other U.S. citizens but pay no federal taxes and cannot vote in elections for the U.S. President or Congress.

▶*Troops patrolling the streets in Haiti. In the 20th century, the island has been ruled by dictators and has suffered from political unrest.*

▼ *An election rally in support of the National Front for Change and Democracy (FNCD), in Port-au-Prince, Haiti.*

is a self-governing commonwealth in a free political association with the U.S., and its citizens are U.S. citizens. The people of the U.S. Virgin Islands are also U.S. citizens and operate a legal system based on U.S. law. In Cuba, the Marxist leader Fidel Castro developed strong links with the former U.S.S.R. and other Marxist leaders in Africa and the Middle East, causing many western nations to impose trade sanctions and halt diplomatic relations with Cuba.

DRUG TRAFFICKING

One of the major law and order issues today is the involvement of some of the islands, such as Dominica, Haiti, Jamaica, and the Netherlands Antilles, in the illegal trafficking of drugs between South America and the U.S. and Europe. Jamaica illegally produces marijuana. The government, with the help of the U.S. Drug Enforcement Agency (DEA), is currently trying to combat this problem.

CASH CROPS

During colonial rule, the development of large-scale commercial farming in the West Indies shaped many of the islands' economies. Today crops such as sugarcane, bananas, coffee, cocoa, citrus fruits, and tobacco are grown on large estates as "cash crops" for the world markets. Sugarcane is the most important crop and is grown on all the large islands and also on Barbados and St. Kitts. In Jamaica, 20% of the land area is devoted to growing sugarcane. The industry employs 60,000 people (7% of the workforce) and generates around 4% of export earnings. Bananas are the region's second major export crop and are particularly important for Dominica,

BANANA PRODUCTION, 1996 (thousand tons)

116	130	135			160
Guadeloupe	Jamaica	St. Lucia			Cuba
210	239	361	5,309	5,692	9,935
Martinique	Haiti	Dominican Republic	Ecuador	Brazil	India

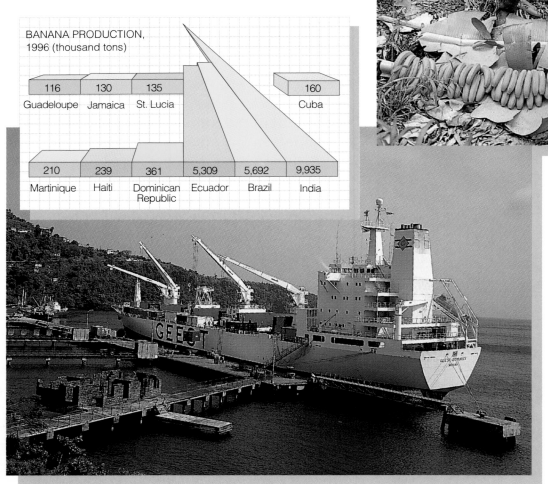

▲ **Cutting bananas for export in St. Lucia. The banana is a large, treelike herbaceous plant, whose thin stem is wrapped in a sheaf of overlapping leaves.**

◀ **The arrival of the large white Geest Industries freighter in Kingstown Harbour is an important weekly event in St. Vincent.**

KEY FACTS

● The weather can seriously disrupt Caribbean agriculture. In 1995, 20% of St. Lucia's banana crop was destroyed by tropical storm Iris, and hurricanes Luis and Marilyn destroyed virtually all of Dominica's banana crop.

● The U.S. Virgin Islands does not have enough farmland to be self-sufficient in food and imports most of its food from the U.S. The Cayman Islands imports around 90% of its food.

● The Dominican Republic produced 46,652 tons of coffee in 1996 and is the region's biggest producer. Jamaica produced only 2,580 tons, but its Blue Mountain coffee is said to be among the best (and most expensive) in the world.

● In 1991 nearly 35% of Haiti's GROSS DOMESTIC PRODUCT (GDP) was from the agricultural sector, and it employed 66% of the island's labor force.

St. Lucia, and St. Vincent. The Dominican Republic and Haiti are the region's leading producers, and in 1996 produced 361,047 and 239,200 tons respectively. St. Lucia produced about 135,000 tons, which accounted for over 50% of its export earnings. It can be risky for an island to rely heavily on a single crop, because world demand can vary, and weather, disease, or pests can destroy the crop. Increased production of bananas in South America has already lowered the market price, and in 1995 many of the islands had their crops partially destroyed in a series of tropical storms.

Spices are an important part of West Indian agriculture. Jamaica is a major producer of allspice, and Grenada is one of the world's largest nutmeg producers. Other spices grown in the region include cinnamon, cloves, ginger, and various peppers. In recent years, West Indian agriculture has expanded into horticulture—the production of fresh fruits, vegetables, plants, and flowers. Jamaica and the Bahamas supply

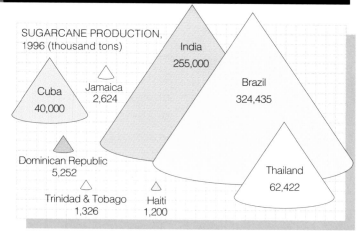

SUGARCANE PRODUCTION, 1996 (thousand tons)

India 255,000

Cuba 40,000

Jamaica 2,624

Brazil 324,435

Dominican Republic 5,252

Thailand 62,422

Trinidad & Tobago 1,326

Haiti 1,200

▶ *Sugarcane at a factory in Jamaica. The cane is washed, shredded, and then crushed to extract the juice. The juice is boiled, and the water evaporates, leaving crystals of brown sugar.*

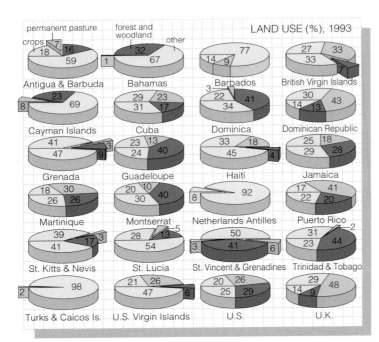

LAND USE (%), 1993

permanent pasture
crops
forest and woodland
other

Antigua & Barbuda: crops 7, permanent pasture 18, forest 16, other 59

Bahamas: 1, 32, 67

Barbados: 77, 14, 9

British Virgin Islands: 27, 33, 33, 7

Cayman Islands: 8, 23, 69

Cuba: 29, 23, 31, 17

Dominica: 3, 22, 41, 34

Dominican Republic: 30, 43, 14, 13

Grenada: 41, 47, 3, 9

Guadeloupe: 23, 13, 24, 40

Haiti: 33, 18, 45, 4

Jamaica: 25, 18, 29, 28

Martinique: 18, 30, 26, 26

Montserrat: 20, 10, 30, 40

Netherlands Antilles: 8, 92

Puerto Rico: 17, 41, 22, 20

St. Kitts & Nevis: 39, 41, 17, 3

St. Lucia: 28, 13, 54, 5

St. Vincent & Grenadines: 3, 50, 41, 6

Trinidad & Tobago: 31, 23, 44, 2

Turks & Caicos Is.: 2, 98

U.S. Virgin Islands: 21, 26, 47, 6

U.S.: 20, 26, 25, 29

U.K.: 29, 48, 14, 9

cucumbers and tomatoes to the North American market, while Puerto Rico and Jamaica have successfully entered the international market for houseplants and flowers.

LOCAL FOOD AND FARMING

The staple foods of the West Indies include yams, cassava, potatoes, sweet potatoes, plantains, breadfruit, and various vegetables. These are normally grown on small farms of up to 7 acres (3 ha) and sold in lively and colorful markets. On the smaller plots, farmers may not produce a surplus for sale, and the family will consume all of what is grown. This is called

◄ *Yams, carrots, cucumbers, tomatoes, pumpkins, and peppers are some of the vegetables offered for sale at markets throughout the West Indies. Food crops are mostly produced by small farmers, who sell their surplus at markets like this.*

◄ *A seine net is drawn in on the beach in Grenada. When a catch is landed, family members help the fishermen to sort and sell the fish. Fishing in the West Indies is insignificant in world terms, but fish are an important part of the local diet.*

SUBSISTENCE FARMING. In Haiti, it accounts for the majority of the 66 percent of the workforce working on the land. Many farmers will grow several crops on their land at the same time, a technique known as INTERCROPPING. This ensures a continuous supply of food throughout the year. It also helps to protect against drought or disease, since some plants will be more resistant than others. Livestock farming is not important in the region, although cattle are kept on Puerto Rico, Jamaica, and Trinidad. Smaller livestock, such as goats, pigs, and chickens, are often kept to meet people's own needs.

Despite being surrounded by sea, most of the region's fish is imported, with only the Bahamas being self-sufficient. The Caribbean Sea lacks nutrients, and the best fishing grounds, such as those around Jamaica, have been overexploited and now provide very few fish at all to eat.

In Caribbean cooking, roots, vegetables, fruits, spices, fish, chicken, and goat are used in a variety of dishes influenced by Indian, African, European, and American tastes. A local snack food, roti, is particularly common. It is a spicy curried filling (often potato and chicken) rolled in a tortillalike bread, which is very inexpensive.

Limited farmland means that much of the Caribbean food for the region is imported. Islands such as the Cayman Islands and the Turks and Caicos Islands rely almost entirely on imported foodstuffs from the United States, United Kingdom, and neighboring islands. Beef and dairy products are particularly scarce and account for about 35% of the import bill. A severe strain can be placed on the economy of a country that is forced to rely on imports for basic needs. This can often lead to large debts.

TRADE AND INDUSTRY

The West Indies are dominated by a single industry—tourism. The tropical climate, friendly people, and beautiful scenery attract millions of tourists every year from all over the world. Puerto Rico and the Bahamas are the main tourist destinations and, in 1994, they attracted over 3 million, and 1.5 million visitors respectively. Tourism is even more important in the smaller islands, such as the Cayman and U.S. Virgin Islands, where it accounts for about 70 percent of GDP. Tourism is still growing rapidly in many islands. This stimulates growth in other sectors that support tourism, such as

▲ *Cruise ships dock at Charlotte Amalie, St. Thomas, in the U.S. Virgin Islands. Each ship brings hundreds of tourists.*

▶ *Dunn's River Falls is Jamaica's main tourist attraction. About a million people visit it every year.*

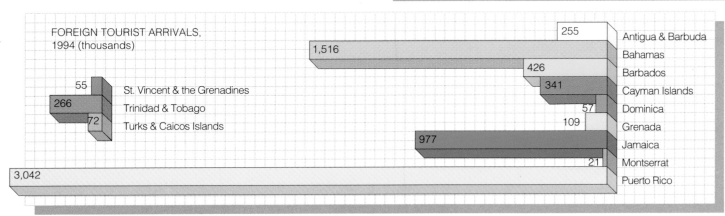

FOREIGN TOURIST ARRIVALS, 1994 (thousands)

Island	Thousands
Antigua & Barbuda	255
Bahamas	1,516
Barbados	426
Cayman Islands	341
Dominica	57
Grenada	109
Jamaica	977
Montserrat	21
Puerto Rico	3,042
St. Vincent & the Grenadines	55
Trinidad & Tobago	266
Turks & Caicos Islands	72

the construction, catering, and transportation industries. As agricultural prices fall, tourist earnings are becoming increasingly important for islands like Martinique and St. Kitts and Nevis.

MANUFACTURING

Manufacturing is expanding in the region but is, so far, limited to a few key industries. Rum is distilled from molasses (a by-product of the sugar industry) on many islands. Cement is produced in Barbados, Cuba, and Trinidad. Jamaica produces alumina, from bauxite, for use in the production of aluminum. One of the biggest industries in the region is the petrochemical industry. Trinidad uses its petroleum resources in the manufacture of detergents, fertilizers, paints, plastics, solvents, and

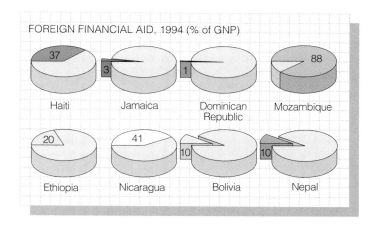

FOREIGN FINANCIAL AID, 1994 (% of GNP)

Haiti	Jamaica	Dominican Republic	Mozambique
37	3	1	88

Ethiopia	Nicaragua	Bolivia	Nepal
20	41	10	10

pharmaceuticals. Other islands, like Jamaica and the U.S. Virgin Islands, have petroleum refineries for the processing of imported oil.

FREE TRADE ZONES have helped to encourage the growth of manufacturing on several islands. Overseas firms are attracted by low wages, the lack of trade

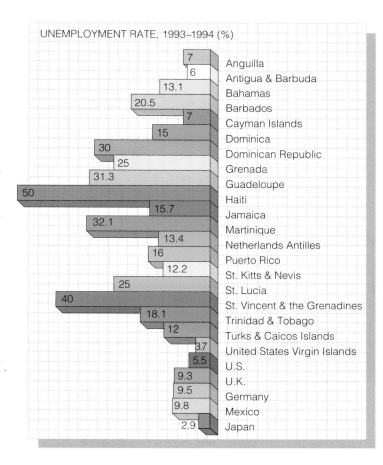

UNEMPLOYMENT RATE, 1993–1994 (%)

Country	Rate
Anguilla	7
Antigua & Barbuda	6
Bahamas	13.1
Barbados	20.5
Cayman Islands	7
Dominica	15
Dominican Republic	30
Grenada	25
Guadeloupe	31.3
Haiti	50
Jamaica	15.7
Martinique	32.1
Netherlands Antilles	13.4
Puerto Rico	16
St. Kitts & Nevis	12.2
St. Lucia	25
St. Vincent & the Grenadines	40
Trinidad & Tobago	18.1
Turks & Caicos Islands	12
United States Virgin Islands	3.7
U.S.	5.5
U.K.	9.3
Germany	9.5
Mexico	9.8
Japan	2.9

▲ *A Rastafarian craftsman making leather boots in St. Kitts.*

▲ *Cloth is painted with wax, as part of the process of making batik, at a small factory in Grenada.*

unions, and low taxation levels. Electronics, textiles, and consumer goods are produced and usually sold in American or European markets. Puerto Rico has the most diverse manufacturing economy, producing more than all the other islands combined. It benefits from close trading relations with the U.S., which means its products are exempt from U.S. import taxes. Companies from the U.S. have also invested heavily in Puerto Rico since the 1950s, making manufacturing its most important sector, and accounting for 42% of GDP.

Offshore financial services are a growing part of economies in the region, particularly in Anguilla, the Bahamas, the Cayman Islands, the Netherlands Antilles, and the Turks and Caicos. These islands are attractive because of their low taxation levels and stable political and economic climates. The Cayman Islands are a particularly important center for financial services, and as a result the people there enjoy one of the highest standards of living in the world today.

IMPORTS AND EXPORTS, 1995 (US$ millions)

imports			exports
653	Barbados	168	
1,868	Guadeloupe	162	
2,773	Jamaica		1,429
1,969	Martinique	242	
1,723	Trinidad & Tobago		2,467

KEY FACTS

● Tourism in the Turks and Caicos islands grew by about 10% in 1995, with most visitors (60,000 or 70%) coming from the U.S.

● Cruise ships are important to Caribbean tourism in the West Indies. In 1994 cruise arrivals in Antigua increased by 17% from the previous year.

● The petroleum refinery at Saint Croix in the U.S. Virgin Islands is one of the largest in the world.

● Jamaica's clothing industry employed 9,000 people in 1984, but by 1994 it had expanded to 44,000. It accounted for US$450 million in export earnings.

● The fall in banana prices in 1993 led to riots in St. Lucia, St. Vincent, and the Grenadines. The changes in the industry are likely to lead to 4,000–8,000 jobs lost on each of the islands.

◀ **The Hato Rey financial area in San Juan, Puerto Rico. Puerto Rico has one of the most dynamic economies in the West Indian region.**

▶ **In Puerto Rico, industry is a more important economic activity than agriculture. This distillery in San Juan produces rum.**

TRADE AGREEMENTS

The West Indies benefit from several trade agreements similar to those of the European Economic Community (EEC) or the North American Free Trade Agreement (NAFTA). The Caribbean Basin Initiative (CBI) allows various Caribbean goods to enter the U.S. market duty-free. The Caribbean Common Market (CARICOM) allows free trade among its member countries. The Organization of the Eastern Caribbean States (OECS), which is made up of Antigua and Barbuda, Dominica, Grenada, St. Kitts and Nevis, St. Lucia, and St. Vincent and the Grenadines, was formed in 1981 as a group within the larger CARICOM. These islands have small populations, a limited land area, and rely heavily on imported goods. They share a common currency (the East Caribbean Dollar) a central bank, and a central planning authority, which means they can compete more effectively in the international markets. One of the recent problems facing the OECS has been the decline in world banana prices since 1992 and the possible loss of the European market for its bananas, after 2001, to South American producers.

TRANSPORTATION

Transportation links are vital to small island economies like those of the West Indies. Shipping is important for the export of minerals and agricultural goods and the import of foodstuffs, consumer goods, and fuel. As the cruise industry expands, the seas also bring hundreds of thousands of tourists every year. Virtually all the islands have ports. The largest ones capable of handling container ships are TRANSSHIPMENT PORTS, such as San Juan in Puerto Rico and Port of Spain in Trinidad. The West Indies are also the main route for shipping traveling through the Panama Canal, which links the Atlantic and Pacific oceans.

Air travel is replacing much of the shipping traffic, particularly for the export of fresh fruits and vegetables and for people traveling both between islands and internationally. Local airports service regional flights operated by several airlines, while the larger

islands such as the Dominican Republic and Haiti have international airports, with connections to the U.S., Europe, and beyond.

Local travel is mainly by road, using buses, trucks, and taxis. The road network

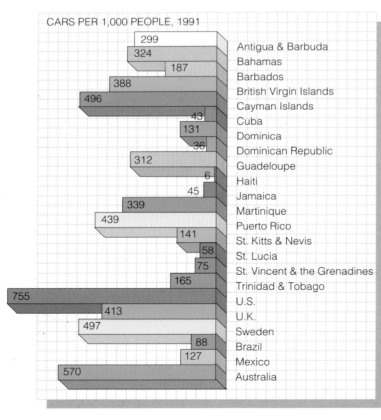

CARS PER 1,000 PEOPLE, 1991

299	Antigua & Barbuda
324	Bahamas
187	Barbados
388	British Virgin Islands
496	Cayman Islands
43	Cuba
131	Dominica
36	Dominican Republic
312	Guadeloupe
6	Haiti
45	Jamaica
339	Martinique
439	Puerto Rico
141	St. Kitts & Nevis
58	St. Lucia
75	St. Vincent & the Grenadines
165	Trinidad & Tobago
755	U.S.
413	U.K.
497	Sweden
88	Brazil
127	Mexico
570	Australia

◀ *Air Jamaica operates over 100 flights a week to the U.S., Canada, and the U.K. Jamaica has two international airports—in Kingston and Montego Bay.*

originally linked the plantations to the ports, but has now expanded to link most towns. The use of private vehicles is limited due to their expense, although wealthier countries, such as the Cayman Islands and Puerto Rico, have a higher proportion of private car use than the United Kingdom. Smaller mountainous states, like Dominica, St. Vincent and the Grenadines, are hampered in their road network by the nature of their landscape, which makes roads expensive to build and maintain.

A few railroads exist to transport goods, such as sugarcane and bauxite, to factories and the ports, but in many cases these are being replaced by road transportation. Only Cuba has a full passenger rail network. For many rural areas, the main means of transportation continues to be by foot or perhaps on donkey, using local footpaths and trails.

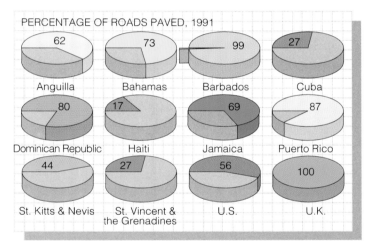

PERCENTAGE OF ROADS PAVED, 1991

Anguilla	Bahamas	Barbados	Cuba
62	73	99	27

Dominican Republic	Haiti	Jamaica	Puerto Rico
80	17	69	87

St. Kitts & Nevis	St. Vincent & the Grenadines	U.S.	U.K.
44	27	56	100

◀ *Girls riding home from the farm on heavily laden donkeys in Haiti*

▶ *Trucks and buses, like this one on St. Kitts, are the most important form of transportation on the islands. They are often dangerously crowded.*

THE ENVIRONMENT

The impact of humans on the environment can be particularly obvious on small islands like those of the West Indies. Where land is limited, population pressure is a major cause of environmental damage. As the population has expanded, the steep slopes of the Yallahs River Basin in Jamaica have been cleared of trees for growing export crops and vegetables for local consumption. This has meant that already serious erosion has worsened and increased the risk of landslides and flooding.

Cutting down trees for firewood and for charcoal production has had a major impact on higher areas of the West Indies, particularly those in Haiti and the Dominican Republic. Antigua and Barbuda, Cuba, St. Lucia, and Trinidad also suffer from high rates of deforestation, as trees are cleared for agriculture, fuel, and tourism development.

Industrial waste is an increasing problem as industry expands throughout the region. Mining, quarrying, and oil refining have left their mark on parts of Cuba, the Dominican Republic, Jamaica, and Trinidad. The waters of the region's main harbors are heavily polluted with industrial waste. This pollution has spread to cause serious damage to coral reefs and beaches in the area, disrupting tourism and killing local fish. Oceangoing tourist liners have also been accused of damaging local marine life.

Fishing in the West Indies has been so intensive that, in many areas, there are actually very few fish left. Fine-meshed nets

▼ *Factories close to the beach in Barbados risk polluting an important tourist resource.*

KEY FACTS

● Dominica's energy is mainly from hydroelectric power. Investment for this and for the water supply system is partly financed by the export of water to drier islands, including Antigua.

● El Yunque is a 27,180-acre (11,000-ha) rain forest, with more than 240 species of trees, in the Luquillo Mountains in Puerto Rico. It is the only tropical rain forest in the U.S. National Forest system.

● The sea around the Bahamas is home to 5% of the world's coral. Coral absorbs carbon dioxide, just as the rain forests do.

● Jamaica has nearly 3,000 varieties of flowering plants, including 800 species found nowhere else in the world. There are 200 native species of wild orchids.

● Every day, about 20 treatment plants dump 14,500,000 gallons (55 million l) of sewage into Kingston Harbour, Jamaica.

● In 1993 Haiti used 21,792 cubic feet (6,171 cubic meters) of local wood for fuel.

and fish pots mean that fish are caught very young, often before they have bred, so that overall stocks are reduced. The technique of blasting fish out of the coral with explosives has also seriously damaged not only fish populations, but also the environment for lobsters and other marine species. In Jamaican waters, the pressures on fishing have been so high that the average fish catch per canoe declined from 5,500 lb. (2,500 kg) in 1981, to just 2,204 lb. (1,000 kg) in 1991.

Freshwater is in very short supply on smaller islands like the British Virgin Islands, the Cayman Islands, and the Turks and Caicos Islands. Many rely on the collection of rainwater for much of their supply. Even larger islands have limited water supplies. Periodic droughts, such as those in Puerto Rico, have sometimes led to water rationing.

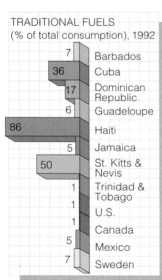

TRADITIONAL FUELS
(% of total consumption), 1992

7	Barbados
36	Cuba
17	Dominican Republic
6	Guadeloupe
86	Haiti
5	Jamaica
50	St. Kitts & Nevis
1	Trinidad & Tobago
1	U.S.
1	Canada
5	Mexico
7	Sweden

▲ *A charcoal kiln in Jamaica. Some practices, such as felling trees for the manufacture of charcoal, contribute to deforestation and soil erosion in many islands.*

▼ *Lush tropical forest and bananas thrive on hillsides like this one in Puerto Rico. Many governments in the region have set up national parks to help protect the environment.*

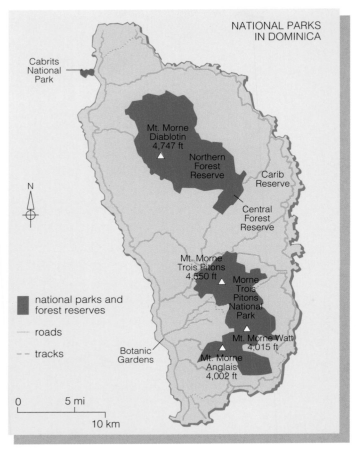

NATIONAL PARKS IN DOMINICA

Cabrits National Park

Mt. Morne Diablotin 4,747 ft

Northern Forest Reserve

Carib Reserve

Central Forest Reserve

Mt. Morne Trois Pitons 4,550 ft

Morne Trois Pitons National Park

Mt. Morne Watt 4,015 ft

Botanic Gardens

Mt. Morne Anglais 4,002 ft

N

■ national parks and forest reserves

— roads

-- tracks

0   5 mi

10 km

CONSERVATION

Despite its problems, the West Indies are largely unspoiled. Large parts still have the wooded mountains, white sandy beaches, and clear seas that give the region its reputation as a tropical paradise. Governments recognize the value of the environment to tourism and of tourism to the economy. They have, therefore, adopted policies to conserve their natural beauty and wildlife for future generations.

National parks are the main means of controlling human activity in fragile habitats. They also protect endangered plant and animal species. Guadeloupe has a 74,128-acre (30,000-ha) rain forest reserve at the foot of La Soufrière. Two-thirds of the deep valleys and most of the shoreline on the U.S. Virgin island, St. John, have been set aside as a national park. Dominica has protected large areas that provide a home to its prolific bird life, including several rare and endangered species. It also has marine parks, as do the Turks and Caicos Islands, where the government has set up underwater parks that protect over 500 miles (800 km) of coral reef. The Jamaican government

▲ *The queen angelfish is one of the many colorful species that inhabit the West Indian reefs.*

◄ *Tobago's blue-crowned motmot is one of Trinidad and Tobago's three national birds.*

established a National Resource Conservation Project in 1991 and works with a nongovernment organization (NGO), the Jamaican Conservation and Development Trust, to protect its habitats and species. Jamaica has also been a leader in the United Nations (UN) International Seabed Authority (ISA), whose aim is to manage marine resources more efficiently. According to the Law of the Sea Convention, which was passed in 1994, the ISA is to be based in Jamaica.

THE FUTURE

The islands of the West Indies have made great progress in the last 50 years, mainly due to favorable trade terms for agricultural exports to the U.S. and Europe. In the 1960s and 1970s, many of the islands' GDPs grew by between 5% and 6% a year. However, in the 1980s, world prices for agricultural and industrial commodities fell. This, together with long periods of worldwide recession, has reversed economic growth in many islands.

Tourism has been growing rapidly since the 1970s, and it continues to bring valuable income to the West Indies. There is, however, some concern about how it may affect the environment and whether it is desirable for some island economies to be so dependent on the tourist trade.

Manufacturing and financial services have, however, begun to expand on many islands. In any case, governments will need to make sure that future development does not harm the natural environment or the limited resources on which many of the island economies rely so heavily.

KEY FACTS

● In the Dominican Republic, life expectancy is likely to rise from 60 years in 1970 to 77 years by 2025.

● The new Barahona International Airport in the Dominican Republic is expected to lead to a rapid growth in tourism along the southwest coast.

● A US$ 28.2 million health and population project, funded by the World Bank and the Inter-American Development Bank, intends to extend health services to Haiti's poor. It aims to reduce cases of tuberculosis by half between 1997 and 2000 and also to help with a national AIDS program.

● Direct Foreign investment into Trinidad and Tobago increased from US$ 63 million in 1988 to US$ 415 million in 1994. Changes to local taxes are expected to increase investment even more in the future.

● In 1997 the World Bank stated that the West Indies must aim to diversify their economies, attract foreign investment, and create jobs. Telecommunications, financial services, high-tech manufacturing, and data processing are all possible growth industries.

● Arecibo Observatory in Puerto Rico is the site of the largest radio telescope in the world.

◄ Students learning keyboard skills. On several islands, data processing and information-based services are new industries with great potential for growth.

FURTHER INFORMATION

● ANGUILLA TOURIST OFFICE
World Trade Center, Suite 25
San Francisco, CA 94111

● ANTIGUA & BARBUDA
Department of Tourism and Trade
25 S.E. 2nd Avenue, Suite 300
Miami, FL 33131

● BAHAMAS CENTER
150 East 52nd St.
New York, NY 10022

● BARBADOS TOURISM AUTHORITY
800 Second Ave.
New York, NY 10017

● CAYMAN ISLANDS DEPARTMENT OF
TOURISM
420 Lexington Ave., Suite 2733
New York, NY 10170

● CUBAN TOURIST BOARD
440 Dorchester Blvd. West,
Suite 1202
Montreal, PQ H2Z 1V7, Canada

● OFFICE OF GRENADA TOURISM
820 Second Ave., Suite 9D
New York, NY 10017

● JAMAICA TOURIST BOARD
801 Second Ave., 20th Floor
New York, NY 10017

● ST. KITTS & NEVIS TOURIST BOARD
414 East 75th Street
New York, NY 10021

● ST. LUCIA TOURIST BOARD
820 Second Ave., 9th Floor
New York, NY 10017

● TRINIDAD AND TOBAGO TOURISM BOARD
7000 Blvd. East
Guttenberg, NJ 07093

● TURKS AND CAICOS TOURISM OFFICE
c/o Trombone Association, Inc.
420 Madison Ave.
New York, NY 10017

● VIRGIN ISLANDS DIVISION OF TOURISM
1270 Avenue of the Americas
New York, NY 10020

BOOKS ABOUT THE WEST INDIES

Brothers, Don. *West Indies.* "Places and Peoples
of the World" series. Chelsea House, 1989.

Mayer, T. W. *The Caribbean and Its People.*
"People and Places" series. Raintree Steck-
Vaughn, 1995.

Ramlin, Ron. *West Indies.* "World in View" series.
Raintree Steck-Vaughn, 1991.

Sunshine, Catherine H., and Menkart, Deborah, eds.
*Caribbean Connection: Overview of Regional
History.* "Classroom Resources for Secondary
Schools" series. Network of Education, 1991.

GLOSSARY

BAUXITE
The ore from which aluminum oxide is extracted. Aluminum is made from this oxide.

COSMOPOLITAN
A word used to describe a population that is a mixture of people and cultures from many different parts of the world.

COUP D'ÉTAT
A violent or illegal change in government.

DEFORESTATION
The clearing of trees by people, either to burn them as fuel or to use the land for a different purpose, such as farming.

FREE TRADE ZONES
Areas that offer financial incentives to attract businesses.

GROSS DOMESTIC PRODUCT (GDP)
A similar measure to GNP, except that GDP does not include money earned by a country from investments abroad.

GROSS NATIONAL PRODUCT (GNP) PER CAPITA
The total value of all the goods and services produced by a country in a year, divided by the number of people in the country.

HYDROELECTRICITY
Electricity produced by flowing water that drives a generator.

INDENTURED LABORERS
People who agreed to work for several years at a set wage in return for their fare.

INTERCROPPING
Growing different crops together, in an irregular pattern, to use the land efficiently.

MULTINATIONALS
Companies operating in several countries. They are normally based in North America, Europe, and Japan.

SALT PAN
A shallow lake of seawater that evaporates to leave salt.

SUBSISTENCE FARMING
Farming that produces only enough food for the family, with little or no surplus produce to sell.

TRANSSHIPMENT PORTS
Major ports where goods are transferred from ships used in local trade to and from larger oceangoing container ships.

TROPICAL KARST
Limestone eroded by underground rivers that collapses and looks like large honeycombs.

TROPICS
The latitudinal region lying between 23.5°N (the Tropic of Cancer) and 23.5°S (the Tropic of Capricorn) of 0° (the equator).

INDEX